Unintentional HUMOR®

Celebrating the Literal Mind®

Volume 2

Brent Anderson &
Linda Gund Anderso~

Cartoons by: Alan J. Lewis

Cover Design by: Brett Bednorz

ISBN: 978-0-9834509-1-7
eISBN: 978-0-984509-2-4

PRINTED IN THE U.S.A.

Gund Publishing, Inc.
PO Box 270742
Louisville, CO 80027
UnintentionalHumor@gmail.com

Books may be purchased directly from the publisher.
Discounted pricing for educational purposes and fundraising use.

Brent Anderson is an expert on humor and the literal mind. A popular inspirational speaker, he touches audiences with his heart-warming journey and honest description of his life with autism. Brent represents what is possible with support, encouragement, and a sense of humor. He is an active participant on the advisory board of Celebrate Autism.

Linda Gund Anderson used her entrepreneurial experience to create Unintentional Humor® with her son Brent. In 2013, she joined her daughter Jenny in starting the non-profit, Celebrate Autism. Their organization empowers young adults with developmental disabilities by providing innovative education based on entrepreneurial concepts so that they can create happier and more productive lives.

Thank you to everyone that supported the success of *Unintentional Humor®* Volume 1 and encouraged us to produce more *Unintentional Humor®* books. It is an amazing process to understand Brent's literal mind and see his thoughts come to life in our original cartoons.

Through our travels we have met many people who have shared their stories of *Unintentional Humor®* with us. Included in this book are suggestions from the following contributors:

Dan Baker (Big Fish in Small Pond), **Nikki Bryant** (In a Pickle), **Emily Januszewski** (Walking on Pins and Needles), **Michael McNeeley** (Bring Home the Bacon, It's Over your Head), **Ed McManis** (Hair on your Chest) and **Larry Rice** (Dust Bunnies).
(Sincere apologies to anyone left off this list)

Unintentional Humor® cartoons are available as hilarious greeting cards, posters, and comical t-shirts. Books are available at discounted prices for educational purpose and fundraising use. All products are available on our website:

www.UnintentionalHumor.com

BookSales@UnintentionalHumor.com

I created Unintentional Humor® to provide Brent a way to use his creativity and keep him engaged with others. I had **no idea** what other amazing outcomes would result from publishing our book.

In the past 2 years, Brent has shared his story with over 10,000 people in 12 states. His presentation is enjoyed by people of all ages, professions, and backgrounds. Brent's ability to explain his challenges through the use of humor is both educational and inspiring. Through these experiences, Brent has discovered his passion for public speaking.

If you would like Brent to speak to your organization, please submit a request through our website or email: Linda@UnintentionalHumor.com

A huge thank you to our creative team: **Brett Bednorz, Alan J. Lewis,** and **Kurt Muzikar;** and to these amazing individuals for their support: **Jenny Anderson, Kevin Fitzgerald, Natasha Guimont, Andrea Mann, Debra Muzikar, Larry Rice, Dr. Andrea Samson, Gary Schwartz, The Arc of Ventura County,** and **Tri-Counties Regional Center.**

Linda

5

We learned that people enjoy the challenge of guessing our original cartoons, so we designed *Unintentional Humor® Volume 2* with a new interactive format.

Cartoons are on the **even numbered pages** and do not have the answers - making the book a hilarious guessing game. The odd numbered pages provide the cartoon's answer, Brent's literal interpretation of the expression, the actual definition, and interesting facts about the word or expression.

We recommend folding the book in half so only the cartoons (even numbered pages) can be seen while you try to interpret the humor of the literal mind.

How did you score?

15 - 29 Correct	More Practice Needed
30 - 45 Correct	You Are A Brainiac
46 - 60 Correct	A Literal Minded Genius

Unintentional Humor® Volume 3 will be published soon!
Please send us your cartoon suggestions:
UnintentionalHumor@gmail.com

For those who
embrace differences
and
love to laugh

Finger Paint
Noun

Brent's Definition: Painting your fingers

Definition: A type of paint that is meant to be applied with the fingers

Origin: American educator Ruth Shaw is credited with introducing finger paint to art education. She was working in Italy when she developed the techniques and materials for finger painting. In 1931, Shaw patented a safe, non-toxic paint and created a factory to produce the paint. She was seen as a pioneer in progressive education who introduced finger painting to adults.

There are many successful artists who are known to only paint with their hands. Painter Tyler Ramsey claims that he never touched a paint brush, but does wear surgical gloves for safety against toxic oil paints. American artist Iris Scott, Chilean artist Fabian Gaete Maureira and Italian artist Paolo Troilo, also paint without brushes.

9

Teacher's Pet
Homophone / Idiom

Brent's Definition: A teacher's dog or cat

Definition: A teacher's favorite student or someone who has gained favor with authority

Origin: This is an American expression, originated in 1914. It describes the person believed to be the teacher's favorite pupil. This person is often disliked by the other students because they think that the "**teacher's pet**" receives special treatment or favoritism by the teacher.

The word "pet" has many meanings, depending on how it is being used.   **Noun:** A domestic or tamed animal kept for companionship. **Verb:** To stroke or pat affectionately. In this expression, it is used as an **adjective**: A person who is loved or indulged, and a personal favorite.

Synonyms: Brown-noser, Backscratcher

11

12

Ants in Your Pants
Idiom

Brent's Definition: A person with ants crawling inside their pants

Definition: Someone who is restless or impatient

Origin: Ants are very busy insects that are always moving around in their colonies. This expression is used to describe someone that cannot sit still - which is how someone would most likely react if they did have ants crawling on them.

A song recorded in 1934 by Chick Webb and his orchestra is titled, "I Can't Dance (I Got Ants in My Pants)." There is also a popular children's game called *Ants in the Pants*.

Interesting: The word "antsy" is used to describe someone who is moving around a lot and cannot sit still.

Synonyms: The fidgets, Heebie-jeebies

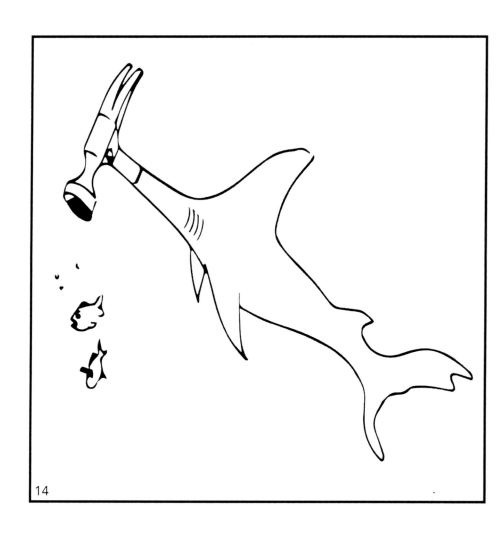

14

Hammerhead Shark
Noun

Brent's Definition: A shark with a hammer on its head

Definition: A group of sharks with unusual, flattened heads

Description: Hammerhead sharks are a group of sharks in the Sphyrnidae family. They have distinct, flattened heads that extend laterally into a "hammer" shape called a cephalofoil. Their unique heads provide a 360° view, meaning they can see what is above and below them at the same time. Most hammerhead sharks are light grey with white bellies helping them blend in well in the ocean. Hammerheads range from 3 to 20 feet in length and can weigh as much as 1,200 pounds. Of the 11 species of hammerheads only 3 have attacked humans, with no fatalities.

Interesting: Unlike most sharks, hammerheads swim in schools during the day and hunt solitarily at night.

Bare Feet
Homophone

Brent's Definition: A person's feet that look like a bear's feet

Definition: Not wearing shoes

Description: This expression is an example of a **homophone**. Two or more words that have the same pronunciation, but different meanings, origins, or spellings.

Bare: A part of a person's body that is not clothed or covered.

Bear: A mammal in the Ursadie family, with common characteristics that include: stocky legs, long snouts, shaggy hair, and paws with five non-retractile claws.

Interesting: There are currently 8 species of bears living in the world.

18

Hit the Road
Verb / Idiomatic Expression

Brent's Definition: A person punching the road

Definition: Someone that is leaving

Description: A slang expression that means you are leaving. The expression is defined as: beginning a journey, traveling, or departing. Whether you walk, bike, drive, or travel by horseback, you are, "**hitting the road.**" This makes sense because most forms of transportation involve making contact with the ground.

The popular song, "Hit the Road Jack" was written by Percy Mayfield and first recorded in 1960. Ray Charles received a Grammy award for his recording of that song in 1961.

Synonyms: Pound the pavement, Split, Take a hike

Goosebumps
Noun

Brent's Definition: A person with bumps that look like geese

Definition: Small bumps on human skin

Description: People regularly get raised bumps on their skin for many different reasons. They can be caused by cold, fear, or feelings of excitement. Some animals also have this same experience, such as porcupines, whose quills raise up when they are threatened. When feathers are plucked out of a goose, the bumps that are left look similar to the raised "**goose bumps**" on human skin.

Other countries have expressions for goosebumps. **Germany:** *Gansehauf* **Finland:** *kananliha* **Italy:** *Pelle d'oca* **France:** *chair de poule* **Poland:** *gesia skorka* **Spain:** *piel de gallina* **Holland:** *kippenvel*

Synonyms: Goose pimples, Goose flesh, Chicken skin

Crazy Glue
Noun

Brent's Definition: A bottle of glue that is crazy

Definition: A very strong glue with the chief ingredient cyanoacrylate

---

Origin: Crazy Glue® is the trademark name for a commercial brand of epoxy glue. It uses a thermosetting resin that is quick drying and very strong. This glue was originally discovered by Dr. Harry Coover in 1942. At the time, Dr. Coover was attempting to make clear plastic gun sights to be used in World War II. Although that was unsuccessful, his glue was a fantastic quick bonding adhesive. In 1958, it was put on the market by Eastman Kodak, where Dr. Coover now worked.

The name Krazy Glue® and pseudo mark Crazy Glue® are registered trademarks of Toagosei Co., Ltd.

Comparable Brands: Super Glue®, Gorilla Glue®

Spill the Beans
Idiom

Brent's Definition: A person who spilled beans

Definition: Telling a secret

Origin: In ancient Greece, people used colored beans for voting. A white bean was used as a positive vote and a black bean for vote against. The voting had to be unanimous, so if the vote collector **spilled the beans** before the final count and a black bean was found, the voting was stopped.

The word 'spill' is quoted in 1574 *Old English Dictionary* as, "to divulge, to let out."

Today, the phrase has the common meaning of upsetting a stable situation by telling a secret.

Synonyms: Upset the applecart, Spill the soup

Rings a Bell
Verb

Brent's Definition: A person ringing a bell

Definition: Something that is familiar

Description: Before electric sirens, bells were used to signal people of an important event. Because bells are very loud, their sound can be heard at great distances and are an effective way to communicate. For most people, the sound of a bell triggers something familiar. Examples include: the doorbell (answer the door), the school bell (time to go to class), church bells (service has ended), a clock bell (the current time).

This expression is often used in the opposite way. When something is unfamiliar people say, "that doesn't ring a bell."

Synonyms: Bring to mind, Strike a note

27

Butterflies in Your Stomach
Idiom

Brent's Definition: A person who has butterflies inside their stomach

Definition: Feeling nervous

Origin: If someone is nervous or has stage fright, they often experience a muscle spasm in their stomach. Some people call this feeling the "flutters." Butterflies are known to flutter their wings, so this feeling may seem as though there are butterflies in your stomach.

This expression was first recorded in the Oxford English Dictionary in 1908, as a light muscle spasm of anxiety. The definition we use today was quoted in *Boys' Life*, February, 1943 by former scout and paratrooper, Bill Gardner, "I landed all right, although I'll always have **'butterflies in my stomach'** every time I go up."

Synonyms: Dithers, Collywobbles

My Nose is Running
Homophone

Brent's Definition: A nose running a race

Definition: To have fluid coming out of your nose

Description: When a person has a "runny" or "running" nose, they are usually suffering from allergies or the common cold. There are a lot of different treatments for this condition, although the most popular are over-the-counter antihistamines.

Other reasons a person may have a "**running nose**":

> Cold Temperatures
> Crying
> Influenza
> Migraine Headaches

Medical Term: Rhinorrhea

Fork in the Road
Metaphor / Homophone

Brent's Definition: A piece of silverware in the road

Definition: A large decision to be made -
A junction in the road that goes two directions

Origin: The word **fork** means to divide into two or more branches. In the Bible, Ezekiel 21:21, "For the King of Babylon will stop at the fork in the road, at the junction of two roads, to seek an omen."

As a metaphor, the expression represents a deciding moment in life when major choices need to be made. The famous 1916 Robert Frost poem, *The Road Not Taken* states, "Two roads diverged in a yellow wood. . . I took the one less traveled by."

Interesting: There are more than 8 songs or albums titled, "Fork in the Road."

Synonyms: Branch out, Diverge

33

Copy Cat
Idiom / Noun

Brent's Definition: A cat making copies

Definition: Someone that imitates another person

Origin: Found in the 1887 book, *Bar Harbor Days*, "Our boys say you are a copy cat, if you write anything that's already printed." Also in Sarah Orne Jewett's 1890 novel, *Betty Leicester: A Story for Girls*, "I wouldn't be such a copy-cat."

The word 'cat' has been used as an negative comment since medieval times. After David Dressler wrote the 1961 article, "Case of the Copycat Criminal," the term has been used to describe certain kinds of criminal activity.

Interesting: Unlike monkeys and parrots, cats are not known for imitative behavior.

Synonyms: Aper, Mimic, Imitator

Team of Horses
Collective Noun

Brent's Definition: Horses playing on a sports team
(such as the Denver Broncos or Indianapolis Colts)

Definition: A group of horses

Description: The word '**team**' is defined as people or animals that work together for a common goal.

Most sports are performed by teams, but there are teams of people participating in other activities, such as; a sales team, a construction team or a debate team.

When two or more horses are harnessed together they are working as a team, therefore a group of horses is referred to as a team.

Interesting: Horses are highly social animals that prefer to live in groups.

Animal Groups in Teams: Team of oxen, Team of seals, Team of cattle, Team of ducks (in flight)

Jaywalking
Noun

Brent's Definition: A blue jay walking across the street

Definition: To cross or walk in the street unlawfully, without regard for approaching traffic

Origin: In the early 1900's, people visiting New York were commonly referred to as "jays," a popular slang term meaning "simpleton." These "jays" were renowned for wandering into traffic as they marveled at the tall buildings and the large number of people in New York. Before long, the habit of crossing the street at inappropriate or dangerous times became known as "**jaywalking**." The expression was first used in print in the *Chicago Tribune* in 1909.

Interesting: A jay is a bird in the crow family. There are 35-40 species of these medium-sized, colorful, and noisy birds.

Important: It is against the law to jaywalk

Dust Bunnies
Noun

Brent's Definition: A type of rabbit

Definition: Clumps of dust that gather under furniture or in areas that are not often cleaned

Origin: First cited as American slang in 1965-1970. These small piles of dirt and dust consist of hair, lint, spider webs, and dead skin. Sometimes they look fluffy (like a bunny rabbit). They often contain dust mites and other parasites so they should not be played with.

Throughout the USA there are a variety of expressions for dust bunnies. 'Dust Kitties' in the Northeast, 'Woollies' in Pennsylvania, and 'House Moss' in the South.

Interesting: There are over 150 names that people use to describe these piles of dust.

Synonyms: Dust ball, Ghost turd, Dust mouse

41

42

Charley Horse
Noun

Brent's Definition: A horse named Charlie

Definition: A painful muscle spasm or cramp usually in the leg muscles

Origin: An American phrase that originated in the 1880's among baseball players. The name Charley is disputed, but probably referred to the name of a lame draft horse that was being used to drag the infield. Some people say it was the name of an injured baseball player who was limping around the field like one of the elderly racehorses.

There are a variety of reasons that people get these painful muscle cramps. Some of the causes include: overuse of a specific muscle, exercising in excessive hot or cold temperatures, low potassium levels, dehydration, or previous muscle injuries.

Synonym: A corked thigh (corky) in Australia

Rat Race
Noun / Idiom

Brent's Definition: Rat's driving cars in a race

Definition: Living in a competitive struggle for wealth or power

Origin: This American expression originated in the 1930's and describes people working long hours as they try to get ahead financially or professionally. This usually results in a destructive, hard-to-break, busy lifestyle that is unhealthy and damaging. The idea of a rat running on a wheel or frantically trying to get out of a maze is what this expression symbolizes.

The phrase is found in author Christopher Morley's 1939 novel *Kitty Foyle*: "Their own private life gets to be a rat race."

Rat Race is frequently used in the media and is the title of a popular 2001 movie.

In the Doghouse
Idiomatic Expression

Brent's Definition: Someone in a dog house

Definition: A person who is in trouble

Origin: This expression is found in the 1926 book, *Criminalese*, J. J. Finerty's glossary of the language of criminals. Also in the 1933 *Waterloo Daily Courier*, "The poor French ambassador! You can't help but feel sorry for him. He is still in the doghouse."

In Chapter 16 of J. M. Barrie's popular book, *Peter Pan* (1911), Mr. Darling went "in the dog's house" to punish himself for allowing his children to be kidnapped.

While the origin may be uncertain, the definition of 'being in trouble' is agreed on.

Synonyms: In hot water, Up the creek

Eyes Bigger Than Your Stomach
Idiom

Brent's Definition: A person with huge eyes

Definition: Taking more food than you can eat, being greedy

Origin: This expression has been used in the English language for over 200 years. It has a variety of meanings, the most common refers to a person that takes more food than they could possibly eat. Figuratively, it describes someone who is greedy and wants more than they can handle. A 1984 *Forbes* magazine article used the expression to describe an investor who lost a lot of money, "Dick's eyes were bigger than his stomach."

A very early use was written in 1580, *Euphues and His England* by John Lyly, "Guard lest the eyes be bigger than the stomach."

Synonyms: Gluttonous, Self indulgent

49

50

Cry Wolf
Idiom / Metaphor

Brent's Definition: A wolf that is crying

Definition: Asking for help when you don't need it

Origin: This expression comes from the famous Greek fabulist, Aesop, who lived from 620-560 B.C.E. He tells the story of a boy who was given the responsibility of watching over the sheep for the night. He grew bored with his assignment and pretended to be in danger by shouting, "wolf, wolf!" Quickly people came to help him, but soon found out he was not telling the truth. He repeated the game a few more times, until people no longer responded to his cries for help. Later, when a wolf actually did show up, people did not believe him and no one came to help.

Important: If you tell lies, eventually no one will believe anything you say.

Band of Gorillas
Collective Noun

Brent's Definition: Gorillas performing in a band

Definition: A group of gorillas

Description: A **band** is a unit of social organization consisting of a small number of families living together, cooperatively. Gorillas usually live in groups of 6 or 12, called "bands" or a "troop." The band is made up of mostly females, led by one dominant male.

Interesting: Gorillas, like humans, are primates. They are shy, social animals that are extremely intelligent. They can learn and listen to basic language. The most famous gorilla is Koko, who understands over 1,000 words in sign language and 2,000 words of spoken English.

Animal Groups in Bands: Band of jays, Band of coyotes

Hold Your Horses
Idiom

Brent's Definition: Holding on to a horse by the reigns or with a rope

Definition: Be patient or slow down

Origin: An American expression, originally printed as "hold your hosses." In 1844, the newspaper *Picayune* wrote, "Oh, hold your hosses, Squire. There's no use gettin' riled, no how." The word "hoss" is a slang term for horse. During the 1800's, most people traveled by horseback or in horse drawn carriages so telling someone to "hold your horses" was the same as telling them to wait.

Before a horse race, riders must "**hold on to their horses**" to keep them from starting before the sounding gun, otherwise they will be disqualified.

Synonyms: Hold everything, Hold on tight, Wait a minute

Bend Over Backwards
Idiom

Brent's Definition: A person doing a back bend

Definition: Go to extreme measures to please or help someone

Origin: This term originated in the USA in the 1920's. It is believed that the expression represents the opposite of what most people do to help others. By doing something that is the opposite of natural instinct, a person is showing a real effort to help and support someone.

In another explanation, acrobats and contortionists often twist themselves into unusual positions to attract attention and win the praise of the audience. In this case, bending over backwards comes with the expectation of receiving a reward.

Synonyms: Go out of the way, Take special pains

Kick the Bucket
Idiom

Brent's Definition: A person kicking a bucket

Definition: To die

Origin: There are a variety of explanations for this expression. It possibly originated in the Middle Ages when people committed suicide by standing on a bucket to hang themselves. If someone kicked the bucket out of the way, they would then die.

In the Catholic church, when someone dies they often put a bucket of holy water at their feet to sprinkle on the body.

The popular expression, the **Bucket List**, refers to things you want to do before you die.

Synonyms: Bite the dust, Buy the farm, Pass away, Go belly up

Hair on Your Chest
Homophone

Brent's Definition: A rabbit sitting on someone's chest

Definition: Hair growing on a man's chest

Description: It is easy to understand why the words **hair** and **hare** are confusing.

Hair: Any of the many fine, keratinous filaments growing from the skin of humans and animals.

Hare: A rodent like animal from the genus, *Lepus*, that has long ears, a divided upper lip and long hind limps adapted for leaping. Most people think that rabbits and hares are the same, but they are not. They are actually a separate species. Hares are larger, have longer ears and are less social than rabbits.

Interesting: Chest hair is 'androgenic hair' that develops on men during puberty.

Big Fish in a Small Pond
Idiom

Brent's Definition: A fish too big for the pond

Definition: An important person in a group that would have less power in a larger organization

Origin: This American phrase was used in *The Galveston Daily* in 1881, "the locals are big fish in a small pond."

In recent years, the expression was researched by Oxford professor Herbert Marsh and popularized by Matthew Gardner and Malcolm Gladwell. The idea suggests that the self-concept of students is correlated with the ability of their peers. If other students are performing lower, then the student will feel better about oneself. This can have the opposite effect when students are performing higher, which is called "the small fish is a big pond" effect.

Synonyms: Big wheel, Big wig, The big cheese

63

Cold Feet
Homophone / Noun

Brent's Definition: A person whose feet are cold

Definition: To be nervous or anxious; to reconsider a decision about an upcoming event

Origin: Since the early 1800's people have used this expression for someone who is lacking courage. It is often used to describe someone who changes their mind about getting married.

Interesting: People often have cold feet when they are frightened or feel threatened. Humans and animals have a built in "fight or flight reflex," that sends blood to the large muscles of the body (heart, legs, and arms) so they can either fight off the danger or run away. When this happens, there is less blood flow to the extremities, resulting in cold hands and feet.

Synonyms: Chicken, Second thoughts, Weak knees

Happy as a Clam
Simile

Brent's Definition: A clam that is happy

Definition: Feeling extremely happy

Origin: This saying is shortened from the original expression, "happy as a clam at high tide." Because clams are much easier to dig during low tide, they are rarely in danger of being harvested during high tide. When they are safe, they are most likely happy.

The 1840 John Saxe poem, *Sonnet to a Clam:*

> *"Inglorious friend! most confident I am*
> *Thy life is one of very little ease;*
> *Albeit men mock thee with their similes,*
> *And prate of being 'happy as a clam!'"*

Synonyms: Over the moon, On cloud nine,
Tickled pink

Get the Monkey Off My Back
Idiom

Brent's Definition: A person carrying a monkey on their back

Definition: Get rid of a problem or bad habit

Origin: This expression refers to a problem that is serious and does not seem that it will go away. It first appeared in the texts of Ancient Sumeria where substance abusers and others social outcasts were marked with a large scarlet monkey. Other literary references from the turn of the century reinforce the idea of the monkey as an evil spirit, that makes someone do something they would not otherwise do.

Interesting: Monkeys do carry their young on their backs, but that doesn't have any value to this idiom.

Synonyms: Thorn in one's side, Ball and chain

Walking on Pins & Needles
Idiom

Brent's Definition: Stepping on pins & needles

Definition: Being very careful, nervous or anxious

Origin: Because it hurts to be stuck by a needle or a sharp pin, walking across a floor covered in pins and needles would require you to move very cautiously.

When blood circulation returns to a part of the body that has been blocked (mostly fingers and toes), it creates a tingling sensation, sometimes called "pins and needles." This expression was used to describe a nervous mental state in the 1800's.

In 1889, Mark Twain's, *A Connecticut Yankee*, "Merlin hesitated a moment or two, and I was on pins and needles during that little while."

Synonym: Walking on egg shells

Sick As a Dog
Simile / Idiom

Brent's Definition: A dog that is not feeling well

Definition: A person who is extremely ill
(most likely with stomach ailment)

Origin: This expression dates back to 1705 and is one of the many references of being "**as sick as**" an animal. Because many illnesses (such as the plague) were spread around the world by animals (rats, birds, and even dogs), it was common to think of animals as carriers of disease.

Most animals, including dogs, will eat almost anything which often causes them to be sick.

This expression is often used to describe humans who are vomiting or have an upset stomach.

Synonyms: Under the weather, Sick as a parrot, Green around the gills

73

It's Over Your Head
Idiomatic Expression

Brent's Definition: Something flying above your head

Definition: Too complicated to understand

Description: The most common use of this expression is when something is too difficult or too complicated for someone to understand.

The word "**head**" has many different meanings, but in this expression it refers to the definition, "aptitude for or tolerance of."

There is another popular phrase, "you're in over your head," which means you have taken on more than you can handle. It can also describe someone that is living beyond their financial resources.

Synonyms: It's all Greek to me, Baffling, Out of your league

75

Bring Home the Bacon
Idiom

Brent's Definition: Buying bacon at the grocery store

Definition: To earn money; be financially successful

Origin: The origin of this phrase is suggested to be from Essex, England in 1104. The story states that a local couple impressed the Prior of Little Dunmow with their marital devotion, and he awarded them a side of bacon.

A more recent use of this expression comes from the sport of boxing, where the term "bacon" refers to one's body. In September 1906, the *New York Post-Standard* reported that fighter Joe Gans received a telegram from his mother: "Everyone believes you will win and you will bring home the bacon." Gans won the match and sent his Mom a check for $6,000 saying that "he had not only the bacon, but the gravy."

Synonyms: Take the cake, Deliver the goods

Something Smells Fishy
Idiom

Brent's Definition: A place that smells like fish

Definition: Something suspicious or the feeling that someone is being dishonest

---

Origin: In *Hamlet (1602),* Shakespeare writes, "something is rotten in the State of Denmark." This translates to mean that something is wrong somewhere.

The term "**fishy**" was first used in 1840 to describe a person suspected of a crime. It comes from the knowledge that fish are wet and slippery and hard to hold on to (like a criminal that gets away).

Interesting: The chemical trimethylamine is released when fish begin to break down, causing old fish to smell awful.

Synonyms: A shady deal, Funny business

Have a Cow
Idiomatic Expression

Brent's Definition: Giving someone a cow

Definition: To overreact to a situation

Origin: An informal American slang expression that originated in the 1950's. The Denton Texas newspaper printed in 1959, "He won't let me watch rock and roll shows, he would 'have a cow' if he knew I watched *77 Sunset Strip*." The saying is believed to have evolved from the British expression, "having kittens" which has a similar meaning.

In the 1980's, the expression was made popular by cartoon character Bart Simpson from the TV show, *The Simpsons*. Most people are familiar with Bart Simpson's trademarked expression, "Don't have a cow, man!"

Synonyms: Freak out, Lose it

Crocodile Tears
Idiom

Brent's Definition: Crocodiles crying

Definition: Fake tears or false grief

Origin: The crocodile was a favorite figure in both ancient Greek and Egyptian folklore. A common tale was told of crocodiles making loud wailing sounds to attract prey. People would draw near to discover what was making the loud sounds and then the crocodile could attack.

British writers such as Shakespeare, Tennyson, and Bacon all used "**crocodile tears**" to suggested insincere sympathy and pretend sorrow.

Interesting: Crocodiles do have a lachrymal gland (like humans) and produce tears to lubricate their eyes and wash away salt.

Heard It Through the Grapevine
Idiom

Brent's Definition: A talking grapevine

Definition: Information that is passed from person to person through informal contact

---

Origin: Samuel Morse invented the telegraph machine in 1844. It was a new way to rapidly communicate news. The term **'grapevine telegraph'** was listed in the U.S. dictionary in 1852, explaining that before the invention of the telegraph machine, most information had been shared informally. This expression is a way to explain that you learned information by word of mouth or by gossip.

Interesting: "I Heard It Through the Grapevine" is a well-known Motown song, recorded by Gladys Knight & the Pips in 1967 and Marvin Gaye in 1968.

Synonyms: Gossip, Rumors

Walking Encyclopedia
Noun

Brent's Definition: A book that is walking

Definition: A person who has a lot of knowledge

Origin: Someone who has a vast array of knowledge on a variety of subjects, concepts, and sciences. This person usually has a lot of information about specific topics. The similar expression, "a walking dictionary" was used by George Chapman in his poem, *Tears of Peace* in 1600.

Encyclopedias were first created over 2,000 years ago. The modern encyclopedia evolved from dictionaries in the 17th century. The worlds largest encyclopedia has 118 volumes and 106,000 pages. Today, many people use electronic (online) encyclopedias, such as Wikipedia.

Synonyms: Smarty-pants, Intellectual, Know it all

When Pigs Fly
Idiom

Brent's Definition: Pigs that are able to fly

Definition: Something that will never happen

Origin: This expression is found in a list of proverbs from the 1616 edition of John Withals's English-Latin dictionary, "Pigs fly in the ayre with their tayles forward." (Pigs fly in the air with their tails forward).

Many countries have a similar version of this expression. **France**: "When chicken have teeth" **Germany:** "On Saint Never's Day" **Italy**: "When donkeys will fly" **Spain:** "When frogs grow hair" **Turkey:** "When fish climb trees."

Interesting: This expression is an **adynaton**. A figure of speech that describes an impossibility.

Synonyms: When it snows in summer, In a blue moon

Bite the Bullet
Verb / Idiom

Brent's Definition: Biting down on a bullet

Definition: To endure something painful or difficult by showing courage

Origin: First recorded by Rudyard Kipling in his 1891 novel, *The Light that Failed*, "Steady, Dickie, steady! said the deep voice inside his ear, and the grip tightened. Bite on the bullet old man, and don't let them think you're afraid."

The expression symbolizes the emotional pain one must endure, rather than the physical pain. Although it is believed that soldiers often clenched a bullet between their teeth to endure the pain of surgery without anesthetic, that theory is not proven.

Synonyms: Take one's medicine, Pay the piper, Face the music, Stand up and take it

91

Butter Me Up
Idiom

Brent's Definition: Putting butter on a person

Definition: To be nice to someone in hopes of getting something from them

Origin: There is an ancient Indian custom of "throwing butterballs of ghee (clarified butter that is used in Indian cooking), at the statues of the gods" to seek favor. Additionally, there is a Tibetan tradition, dating to the Tang Dynasty (618-907 A.D.), of creating butter sculptures for the New Year in the belief that such offerings would bring peace and happiness for the full lunar year. The 1816 Old English word, "buterian" is defined as "to flatter lavishly."

Regardless of the origin, it is a common belief that doing something nice, in hopes of getting something in return is, "**buttering someone up.**"

Synonyms: Sweet talk, Play up to, Kiss up

Lose Your Marbles
Slang Expression

Brent's Definition: A person who lost their marble collection

Definition: To lose your mind

Origin: From the 19th century, the term "marbles" was used to mean personal effects or goods. The French word "meubles" means furniture.

This expression was printed in the 1886 *St. Louis Globe-Democrat*, "He has roamed the block all morning like a boy who had lost his marbles." A few years later, **"losing one's marbles"** began to mean being frustrated or angry, and in 1898 the *Portsmouth Times* referred to marbles as a synonym for mental capacity. The 1927, *American Speech* printed, "there goes a man that doesn't have all of his marbles" (mentally deficient).

Synonyms: Go bananas, Flip out, Go crazy

Get Your Goat
Idiom

Brent's Definition: Going to the farm to buy a goat

Definition: To make you annoyed or angry

Origin: This is an American expression, first used in print in 1909. It is believed that people used to put goats in the stalls with racehorses to keep them calm before a race. When the goat was taken away, the horse often became very upset.

Interesting: The goat is a metaphor for your state of peacefulness. It is said that when your goat is with you, you are calm, but if your goat is taken away, you become angry and upset.

Synonyms: Rub the wrong way, Drive me up the wall

The Straw That Broke the Camel's Back
Idiom/Proverb

Brent's Definition: A camel with a broken back

Definition: A minor action that causes a large and sudden reaction

Origin: This is a long known expression that has evolved through the years. Written in 1677 as, "Tis the last feather that breaks the horse's back." It explains how one small addition to a person's burden, when combined with all of the rest, can make it unbearable.

It is not one single piece of hay that overwhelms a camel carrying a load through the desert, it is the total weight of all he is carrying that prevents him from walking any further.

Synonyms: The last straw, Tip the scales, Pushed over the edge

65 LIMIT

Riding Shotgun
Verb

Brent's Definition: A person riding on a gun

Definition: Sitting next to the driver in a car

Origin: This term is derived from the expression "shotgun messenger," which originated in the days of stagecoach travel. If the stagecoach was traveling with cargo (a strongbox), then it required someone riding along with the driver, who carried a shotgun for protection against bandits. If the stagecoach only had passengers, then there was no need for another person "**riding shotgun**."

Interesting: Today, this is a popular game used to determine who is allowed to sit in the front seat next to the driver. With the car in sight, the first person to shout the word "shotgun" wins.

In a Pickle
Idiom

Brent's Definition: Someone inside a pickle

Definition: In a difficult predicament or an undesirable situation

Origin: This phrase dates back to the 1600's. It was used by William Shakespeare in the play, *The Tempest,* in 1611. "I have been in such a pickle since I saw you last that, I fear me, will never out of my bones." In Shakespeare's play, being in a pickle referred to being drunk.

The definition of the word "**pickle**" comes from the Dutch "pekel" which referred to pickling brine or spicy sauce. (If you were stuck in pickling brine or spicy sauce, you would definitely be in a bad situation).

Synonyms: In a tight spot, Up the creek, On the hot seat

Eat Your Words
Verb / Idiom

Brent's Definition: Eating alphabet soup

Definition: To admit you said or did something wrong

Origin: The famous British Prime Minister Winston Churchill said, "In the course of my life, I have often had to eat my words, and I must confess that I have always found it a wholesome diet." (circa 1940's)

"Keep your words sweet, otherwise you may have to eat them," was said by Quaker missionary Stephen Grellet (1773-1855).

Important: If you make an overconfident comment and are proven to be wrong, you will need to apologize and "**eat your words.**"

Synonyms: Eat crow, Humble pie

Kill 2 Birds With 1 Stone
Idiom

Brent's Definition: A person who uses stones to kill birds

Definition: To achieve two things with one action

Origin: In the Greek mythological tale, Daedalus and his son Icarus are held captive in a high tower. They see high walls around them and large birds overhead, awaiting their demise. Daedalus devises a plan to throw stones at the birds in the hope of fashioning artificial wings to enable them to fly home. He throws his stone with a clever motion and is able to strike one bird and with the ricochet, hit a second bird, thus killing two birds with one stone.

Interesting: Today, this expression can be a complimentary way to describe someone who is able to solve two problems with one solution.

Synonym: One fell swoop

On the Same Page
Idiom

Brent's Definition: People reading the same page of a book

Definition: Thinking alike or in agreement

Origin: This is a newer expression, that is believed to have come from an older idiom, "I don't think we're reading from the same hymn sheet."

Printed in the *New York Times* on January 18, 1979, "One of the things that happens when you make as many rule changes as the National Football League has had a propensity to do in the last couple of years, is that it takes a long time for everyone to **get on the same page** as far as the rules are concerned."

Synonyms: Great minds think alike, We are on the same wavelength, Preaching to the choir

110

Sweating Like a Pig
Simile / Metaphor

Brent's Definition: This is impossible, so people should not say it

Definition: To sweat profusely

Origin: This term came from the ancient process of iron smelting. After the smelter heated the iron ore to extreme temperatures, the ore was transferred into a mold that created "pig iron." (The mold resembled a sow with her piglets). When the air cooled around the metal, droplets formed on its surface, causing the look of sweat. When the "**pigs**" "**sweat**" the metal is cool enough to transport.

Interesting: This expression makes no sense to Brent (and many others), because pigs actually don't sweat. They do not have sweat glands and must roll in mud or cool liquid to lower their body temperature.

Synonyms: Sweating buckets, Sweating bullets

Cut the Mustard
Idiom

Brent's Definition: Cutting a mustard container

Definition: Good enough or adequate

Origin: In the Old English craft of mustard making, the Mustardeer (chief mustard maker), would inspect the oak barrels full of mustard by cutting through the thick, leathery top layer to see if it was ready for sale. If the knife was too dull to cut through the top layer, the Mustardeer said the knife "did not cut the mustard."

Some believe the expression was derived from the idiom "pass muster," an expression used for assembling military troops for inspection.

This saying is found in an O. Henry story in 1902, "So I looked around and found a proposition that exactly cut the mustard."

Synonym: Make the grade

Too Many Irons in the Fire
Idiom

Brent's Definition: Putting clothing irons into a fire

Definition: Doing too many things at one time

Origin: This expression dates to the 1500's and comes from the Blacksmith trade. Blacksmiths shape rods of iron by heating them in the fire until they are red-hot and malleable, then hammering them into shape.

Most blacksmiths are working with multiple pieces of iron at the same time. However, if they have too many pieces in the fire at once, they run the risk of ruining them.

Important: Doing too many things at the same time can have bad results.

Synonym: Having too much on your plate, Burning the candle at both ends

A Bone to Pick
Idiom

Brent's Definition: Picking a bone for your dog

Definition: An issue that needs to be discussed and resolved between people

Origin: This dates back to the 1600's and refers to a dog that is continuously chewing on a bone in order to pick it clean and get every single bit of meat off of it.

This expression is used to describe a topic or issue that people spend considerable time arguing or debating, until they have exhausted the subject and there is nothing left to talk about.

It is similar to the phrase "a bone of contention," which describes a dispute between people and refers to two dogs fighting over the same bone.

Synonyms: Squabble, Brannigan, Face-off

Going Dutch
Idiomatic Expression

Brent's Definition: People wearing Dutch clothes

Definition: Two or more people paying for their own meals

Origin: This phrase most likely comes from Dutch etiquette, where it is common for people to pay their own way, even when they are dating. After the 1600's when Dutch immigrants came to America, people began recognizing the idea of paying for oneself as a "Dutch."

Other cultures have phrases to mean the same thing. **Italy**, "pagare alla romana" (pay like they do in Rome), **South America**, "pagar a la Americana" (pay American style) and **France**, "faire moite-moite" (each pays half of the bill).

Synonyms: Dutch treat, Dutch lunch

The Bee's Knees
Idiom

Brent's Definition: This doesn't make sense, bees don't have knees

Definition: Something that is excellent

Origin: In the late 18th century, this expression referred to something that was small or insignificant. It showed up in America in the 1920's as a nonsense expression to denote something excellent. It may have evolved from the expression, **"The be-all and end-all"** (from Shakespeare's *Macbeth*), which was eventually shortened to the "B's and E's." This sounds a lot like "Bee's Knees."

Today, it refers to an outstanding person or thing.

Interesting: Bees carry pollen back to their hive in sacs on their legs.

Synonyms: The cat's pajamas, Peachy keen

Fly by the Seat of Your Pants
Idiom

Brent's Definition: A person flying a plane with their backside

Definition: Figuring out what to do as you go rather than planning ahead

Origin: This is an aviation expression that originated in the 1930's when aircraft had very few navigation aids and flying was mostly accomplished by using the pilot's judgment. On July 19, 1938, the *Edwardsville Intelligencer* described pilot Douglas Corrigan as an aviator **"who flies by the seat of his pants."** Corrigan had submitted a plan to fly from Brooklyn to California but instead ended up in Dublin, Ireland. He said that his compass had failed, but many people think he flew the 29 hours intentionally. He became known as "Wrong Way Corrigan."

Synonyms: Wing it, Play it by ear

Rain on My Parade
Idiom

Brent's Definition: Raining during a parade

Definition: To ruin someone's fun or something special

Origin: This phrase originated from a popular 1964 song titled, "Don't Rain on my Parade," written by Bob Merrill and composed by Jule Styne. The song was sung by Barbra Streisand in the musical *Funny Girl*.

After the song was introduced, people began frequently using the expression. In 1969 it was written in *Mademoiselle* magazine, "when five members of Parliament drop into Boston unexpectedly, the sound system was lost and it looks like it might **rain on her parade**, she'll need the extra time."

Synonym: Spoiler

Thinking Outside the Box

Idiom / Metaphor

Brent's Definition: Sitting outside and thinking

Definition: To think freely and imaginatively

Origin: This is a modern phrase from the 1970 - 1980's, often used in business.

The "box" describes older, more traditional practices. It is thought to be based on solving the "9 dots puzzle," which requires a person to connect 9 dots with 4 straight lines without lifting the pencil. Solving the puzzle requires creative thinking.

Someone that does not conform to older ideas and uses their imagination and creativity to come up with new ideas is described as "**thinking outside the box.**"

Synonyms: Creative, Innovative, Unconventional, Imaginative

Glossary

Unfold this page to cover
cartoon answers